Kana de Manga
Special Edition

JAPANESE SOUND FX!

MANGA UNIVERSITY presents...

JAPANESE SOUND FX!

Created by Glenn Kardy   Art by Chihiro Hattori

TOKYO   SAN FRANCISCO

Manga University Presents ... Kana de Manga Special Edition: Japanese Sound FX!

Published by Manga University under the auspices of Japanime Co. Ltd., 3-31-18 Nishi-Kawaguchi, Kawaguchi-shi, Saitama-ken 332–0021, Japan.

www.mangauniversity.com

ISBN-13: 978-4-921205-12-6
ISBN-10: 4-921205-12-4

y10 11 12 13 14 15 10 9 8 7 6 5 4 3 2

Printed in Canada

CONTENTS

INTRODUCTION

Shhhhhh! Hear that noise?

カタカタ. カタカタ. Kata-kata. Kata-kata.

There it is again! The sound echoes through the halls late at night here at Manga University. What could it be?

A giant robot from one of our books, come to life to torment its creators? No, that would sound more like ガーガー (gaa-gaa), possibly with an explosive ドーン (dōn) or two thrown in.

Still, the sound continues.

カタカタ. カタカタ. Kata-kata. Kata-kata.

Could it be the rain? Certainly not, for we all know that would dance on the rooftops with a gentle しとしと (shito-shito).

No, it's the sound of a lone Manga University professor, working on this very text late into the night, the *tap-tap-tapping* of the keys on a computer keyboard – a noise that sounds like kata-kata in Japanese!

And it's also your first lesson in the rich and colorful world of ぎせいご (giseigo), or Japanese sound effects – those funny-looking words that decorate the backgrounds of all your favorite manga.

But their use isn't limited just to comic books. In fact, sound effects play such an important role in the Japanese language that they have their own special categories: ぎおんご (giongo), for words that represent voiced sounds; ぎたいご (gitaigo), which are onomatopoeic words that represent feelings; and finally ぎじょうご (gijōgo), onomatopoeic descriptions of psychological conditions.

Let's compare those words for a moment to that fun but clunky and hardly common word we use in English, "onomatopoeia." It's not even easy to pronounce – that alone should tell you where it ranks in our language as opposed to the role giseigo plays in Japanese!

Of course, English is not without its common onomatopoeia. We can type with a *tap-tap-tap,* a giant robot can approach with a *stomp-stomp-stomp,* and rain may fall with a steady *pitter-patter.*

However, the steady or even heavy use of these words, so natural in Japanese, is unusual in English. (When there are English-language equivalents for the Japanese sound effects in this book, though, we have highlighted those words by putting them in italics.)

But that's all academic, and while we are here to study the language, we are also here to have fun! Don't worry too much about these categories; there won't be a test, and knowing which words fall into which groups won't increase your understanding.

As long as you pay attention, you will soon be able to look at that happy couple in the Manga University student lounge and know they are in らぶらぶ (rabu-rabu; love). Your pet pooch will greet you wish a friendly わんわん (wan-wan; woof-woof) as you arrive home. And the gentle ぐぅきゅるるる (guukyururururu; rumble) coming from your tummy will tell you it's time for a well-deserved after-school snack!

HIRAGANA AND KATAKANA IN MANGA

To fully enjoy this special edition of *Kana de Manga,* you should be familar with hiragana and katakana, or what we like to call "The ABCs of Japanese." If you aren't, you can still learn plenty from this book, as all of the Japanese words are also written in romaji, or "roman" letters. But determined students are encouraged to read the original *Kana de Manga* first.

Those of you who already have studied *Kana de Manga* will remember that hiragana is used to write Japanese words, while katakana is reserved for foreign words.

In Japanese comics, however, sound effects are written in both hiragana and katakana, even though the words are, strictly speaking, "Japanese." The decision whether to use hiragana or katakana is largely an artistic one; onomatopoeia that are soft and pleasant are usually written in cursive hiragana, while the more angular katakana is favored for sound effects that are loud, harsh, threatening or strong.

NOTES ON THE USE OF ROMAJI

Charts of all standard and modified hiragana and katakana characters, along with their romaji transliterations, can be found on the inside front and back covers of this book.

Long vowels written in hiragana as ああ, いい and うう are romanized as aa, ii and uu, while those written as ええ, おお and おう are romanized as ē, ō and ō, respectively. Elongated vowels indicated by a long dash (ー) in katakana are romanized the same way.

Manga artists also use long dashes in katakana (and occasionally hiragana) to indicate the tripling, quadrupling, etc., of vowel sounds. So while this book romanizes a giant robot's ガーガー as gaa-gaa, it probably sounds more like gaaaaaaaa-gaaaaaaaa. When space permits, artists draw the dashes particularly long to suggest the duration of the sounds.

Artists will also add a small っ or ッ to the end of a sound effect as a visual cue to readers that the word has a little "oomph" at the end. In this book, these kana are ignored when the word is romanized. Thus, the ニャーッ (angry *meow*) of a cat is transliterated as nyaa, not nyaatsu.

This is not to be confused with the small っ or ッ that is placed before another kana character to indicate the doubling of a consonant. For example, きっぷ (ticket) is romanized as kippu, and ノック (knock) is romanized as nokku.

Finally, the ん sound is usually romanized as the letter n. However, when it appears before a "b or "p" sound, the ん is romanized as the letter m. Examples: ごめん (gomen; sorry); にんげん (ningen; human being); しんぶん (shimbun; newspaper); しんぱい (shimpai; worry).

And with that, let your studies continue with a steady せっせと. That's "sesseto" – the sound of hard work!

Animal
sounds

どうぶつ にかんする **Onomatopoeia**

Animal

Bear

ガオー / がおー

Gaō

Old McDonald had a farm, E-I-E-I-O. And on his farm he had some bears, E-I-E-I ... WHOAH! That's one brave farmer! The *roar* of a grown くま (kuma; bear) is written in katakana, while the *growl* of a こぐま (koguma; cub) is written in hiragana (for a less-ferocious sound).

のっしのっし

Nosshi-nosshi

If a bear takes a stroll in the woods, and nobody is around, does it make any noise? What a silly, Zen-like question! Of course it does! It's のっしのっし, which is the sound of lumbering footsteps.

Animal

Bee

ブーン

Buun

The *buzz* of a はち (hachi; bee) usually spells trouble, especially if you're afraid of being stung. And if you hear a whole chorus of すずめばち (suzumebachi; killer bees) singing ブーンブーンブーン, you better make a beeline for the nearest hiding place!

プーン

Puun

The hard "b" sound in ブーン takes on a softer "p" sound in プーン to describe the *buzz* made by smaller flying insects, such as mosquitoes and gnats. Quick, grab a fly-swatter! ぐちゃ (gucha; *splat*)!

Animal

Bird

チチチ

Chi-chi-chi

Two little birds, sitting in a tree, チチチチチチ. The delightful *tweet-tweet-tweet* of songbirds is the first sign that はる (haru; spring) has arrived and love is in the air. As you listen to them *chirp* away and watch them flit about, your own problems may seem to disappear!

カア

Kaa

The カア, or *caw*, of a からす (karasu; crow) is identical in Japanese and English. And in both languages, it's harsh on the ears. Not all birds were born to be かげき (kageki; opera) singers!

Animal

Cat

ニャーッ

Nyaa

Look at what the ねこ (neko; cat) dragged in! To express its frustration with that fresh fish, this cat lets loose with an angry *meow*. The kinder, gentler form of ニャーッ is にゃあ (nyaa; *mew*). And when a feline is feeling fine, it begins to ぐるるぐるる (gururu-gururu; *purr*).

フーッ

Fuu

きをつけて (ki o tsukete; be careful) – this is one crazy こねこ (koneko; kitty)! The arched back! The raised fur! That *hiss*! フーッ! Don't cross her path, or you're likely to get scratched!

Animal

Cow

もおー

Moō

Cows sound pretty much the same in both Japanese and English, though the familiar *moo* is more like "moh" in Nihongo. Incidentally, many うし (ushi; cows) end up on the menu at "Mo-Mo Paradise," a popular Tokyo steakhouse. How's that for delicious irony?

ブフーッ

Bufuu

That powerful ブフーッ, or *snort*, tells us this bitter おうし (oushi; bull) is ready to charge! Perhaps he's ready for some とうぎゅう (tōgyuu; Japanese-style bullfighting), which pits bull against bull (rather than bull against man).

Animal

Dog

わんわん

Wan-wan

Man's best friend is also one of his nosiest. The *woof-woof, ruff-ruff* and *bow-wow* sounds we associate with いぬ (inu; dogs) of all shapes and sizes is taken care of by one in Japanese, わんわん, which also happens to be the word Japanese children use for "doggy."

ガルルル

Garururu

A dog's bark may be worse than its bite, but there's no reason to tempt fate, especially if that hound is *grrrrrowling*! The two sound somewhat similar in English and Japanese, though their is no "ing" ending on the Japanese ガルルル.

Animal

Frog

ゲロゲロ

Gero-gero

He may not look like royalty – ゲロゲロ – but if you have the guts to give this かえる (kaeru; frog) just one little kiss – ゲロゲロ – he'll turn into a Japanese prince. Honest! The Japanese *ribbit,* incidentally, can also be heard as ケロケロ, without the hard "g." Now, pucker up!

ピョーン

Pyōn

When a tadpole grows up and is ready to leave the family lily pad, he does it with an emphatic ピョーン. That's the Japanese onomatopoeia for leaping or bouncing; in English, we use the word *boing* to describe the same sound.

Animal

Horse

ヒヒーン

Hihiin

A horse is a horse, of course, of course, and no one can talk to a horse, of course, but a horse can speak Japanese, of course ... OK, OK. The point we're trying to make is that if Mr. Ed had an Asian accent, his *neigh* would sound more like ヒヒーン than a *whinny*. Giddyap!

パカッパカッ

Paka-paka

The speedy *clippity-clop*, or パカッパカッ, of hooves is a familiar sound along the coastline of Japan's Miyazaki Prefecture, where やせいのうま (yasei no uma; wild horses) are free to run like the wind.

Animal

Monkey

キキー

Kikii

This little guy speaks no evil, but he sure does make a lot of noise! And let's face it – whether it's the familiar *aah-aah ooh-ooh eeh-eeh* sound of a circus さる (saru; monkey), or the more exotic キキー of a にほんざる (nihonzaru; Japanese macaque), simian sounds are just plain silly.

ウホウホ

Uho-uho

Here's a fellow who doesn't have time for monkey business. He's got more serious things on his mind – like becoming king of the ジャングル (jyanguru; jungle). Just listen to this big ape talk. ウホウホ – that's the voice of authority!

Mouse

チュウチュウ

Chuu-chuu

If you hear a *squeak-squeak* coming from the walls of your home, it can only mean one thing – time to get a cat! Japan's most famous ねずみ (nezumi; mouse), by the way, is the electrifying Pikachu, whose name combines the word ピカ (pika; flash) with チュウ (chuu; squeak).

チュウウウ

Chuuuu

When you want to show extreme agitation, just do what our artist has done and turn the mousy word into a strong one. Here, the drawn-out チュウウウ shows us that the mere thought of a cat has these mice shaking with fear.

Animal

Pig

ブー

Buu

The Japanese word for "pig" is ぶた (buta). And when a Japanese pig goes *oink*, it sounds as though it's trying to say its name, only unable to spit out the second syllable. Piglets, by the way, are called こぶた (kobuta; literally, "small pig").

ブヒブヒ

Buhi-buhi

Our artist has humanized this hog by standing it up on two feet, and its ブヒブヒ is much more charming than the ブーブー of the typical porker. Can you say かわいい (kawaii; cute)?

Animal

Rooster

コケコッコー

Kokekokkō

If it walks like a rooster and *cock-a-doodle-doos* like a rooster, then it must be a rooster. Unless it's a Japanese おんどり (ondori; rooster), in which case it keeps the *cock-a* (コケ) part but drops the *doodle-do* in favor of コッコー.

ピヨピヨ

Piyo-piyo

Look at these cute little ひよこ (hiyoko; chicks)! They call for their feed, some attention, and engage in general chickadee socialization with a constant ピヨピヨ, or *chirp-chirp*.

Animal

Sheep

メエメエ

Mē-mē

Sound-effect words that start with a hard "b" are not very pleasant to Japanese ears. Therefore, it makes sense that the *baa-baa* of a gentle herd of ひつじ (hitsuji; sheep) is represented by the softer メエメエ sound in Japanese.

メエー

Meē

Being a cute creature doesn't always earn the animal a softer sound. Here, a loveable little やぎ (yagi; goat) gives a slightly longer メエー than the sheep above, but one *baa* is as good as another!

Human
sounds

にんげん にかんする **Onomatopoeia**

Human

Anger

プンプン

Pun-pun

Manga hath no fury like a woman scorned! When this gal goes プンプン – *hmmmph* – it's over. Our little friend can beg for forgiveness, but it's clearly not helping. Sorry, pal. Here's じゅうえん (juuen; a 10-yen coin). Call someone who cares!

イライラ

Ira-ira

There are lots of things that can make a girl おそい (osoi; late) for a date. It doesn't matter, though – from the いらいら, or *grrrrr,* you know this guy's already upset. She better have a good excuse!

Human

Applause

ぱちぱち

Pachi-pachi

すばらしい (subarashii; wonderful)! Bask in the applause as everyone gives you a hand – you've earned it. We still don't know the sound of one hand clapping – but the sound of many hands going *clap-clap* is ぱちぱち in Japanese.

パンッパンッ

Pam-pan

There is a special kind of clapping done at Shinto shrines. When facing a やしろ (yashiro; shrine), it is customary to clap パンッパンッ, bow, and clap again. These are sharp claps with a brief pause in between them.

Baby talk

ばぶーばぶー

Babuu-babuu

Even before they speak their first "real" words, あかちゃん (akachan; babies) have a language all their own. So if you think *goo-goo gaa-gaa,* or ばぶーばぶー, is mumbo-jumbo, think again. It means, "Feed me, change my diaper, and start saving for my college education!"

ハイハイ

Hai-hai

Watch that kid go! Every babysitter knows how fast toddlers can get into trouble, especially when they've figured out how to crawl – ハイハイ – under the radar!

Human

Bowing

ぺこぺこ

Peko-peko

ごめんなさい (gomen nasai; I'm sorry)! Whatever he did, he's hearing about it from the せんせい (sensei; teacher). And he can ぺこぺこ all morning, but from the looks of things, he's going to have to go beyond bowing and into outright groveling soon!

ぺこり

Pekori

In the West, friends and new acquaintances greet one another with handshakes. In Japan, they bow. The sound of a relaxed, casual おじぎ (ojigi; bow) is described as ぺこり.

Human

Chatting

ぺちゃくちゃ

Pecha-kucha

These two women are having a great time catching up on the latest せけんばなし (sekenbanashi; gossip), but to the bored little girl, it's just mom and her friend going ぺちゃくちゃ, or *yakety-yak*, for what seems like an eternity.

ベラベラ

Bera-bera

Wow. The boss is really talking up a storm! This is the kind of one-sided conversation so incessant that you stop hearing the individual words, and the collective sound turns into an endless べらべら, or *blah-blah-blah*.

Human

Chewing

バリバリ

Bari-bari

Yum! Japanese おせんべい (osenbei; rice crackers) are the best! They are often given as おみやげ (omiyage; travel gifts) by friends returning from a trip. The *munching, crunching* sound of crackers and cookies is バリバリ. Bet you can't eat just one!

ガリガリ

Gari-gari

The hard "g" is a little harsher to Japanese ears than a "b," so ガリガリ signifies a less pleasant sound – the heavy, hard chewing of cubes of こおり (kōri; ice), for instance.

Human

Crying

しくしく

Shiku-shiku

Aww, don't worry. She'll be OK. しくしく is the sound of a feminine sob, similar to *boo-hoo-hoo* in English. If your タイミング (taimingu; timing) is right, you can be there to comfort her. Just don't break her heart, or you'll set off a new round of whimpering!

うわーん

Uwaan

Some tears, of course, have absolutely nothing to do with ハートブレイク(haatobureiku; heartbreak). Babies, for instance, release a mighty *waaaahhh*, or うわーん, when their needs are not being met.

Human

Depression

ずううううううん

Zuuuuuun

There's that sinking feeling: ずううううううん. Looks like this girl just got her test scores, and they're terrible. You can almost hear her spirit being drained with that sound. The more う you add, the worse it gets. ずうううううううううううううううううううううううううううん. See?!

ズーン

Zuun

Looks like he's got a headache THIS BIG. The ズーン sound here matches that of ずつう (zutsuu), the Japanese word for "headache." Time to get some くすり (kusuri; medicine).

Human

Drinking

ゴクゴク

Goku-goku

If ゴクゴク sounds a lot like *gulp gulp*, it's because they represent they very same noise: the draining of a ドリンク (dorinku; drink). But don't go looking for a Big Gulp – the Japanese aren't particularly fond of super-sized soft drinks.

ズズー

Zuzuu

ゴクゴク is fine for cold beverages, but not quite right when drinking りょくちゃ (ryokucha; Japanese green tea). Take it easy, or you'll burn your mouth. Give it a polite ズズー – *sip* – instead.

Human

Eating

もぐもぐ

Mogu-mogu

She may look like a slender gal, but boy does she have a healthy しょくよく (shokuyoku; appetite)! With a steady もぐもぐ, or *munch-munch,* she manages to clean her plate in ladylike fashion. (Unlike our friend at the bottom of this page!)

ガツガツ

Gatsu-gatsu

ガツガツ. Look at him go! He must be はらぺこ (harapeko; starving). Even if you had no idea what this one meant, the way it's written in the illustration lets us know: this is not a quiet, gentle eater!

Human

Exhaustion

ゲッソリ

Gessori

Some Japanese sound effects are perfect. With ゲッソリ, you can practically hear the spirit leaving the body. And if that doesn't make the point, see how our victim has been drawn – as though he has been drained by a きゅうけつき (kyuuketsuki; vampire)!

ぐったり

Guttari

If ゲッソリ is a draining of the spirit, when one is literally worn out to the point of complete exhaustion, the Japanese use ぐったり. No one said Manga University would be easy!

Human

Fever

ゾクゾク

Zoku-zoku

If shivers and chills are making your body go ゾクゾク, you probably have a ねつ (netsu; fever). In Japan, it's good form to wear a surgical mask when you're feeling ill so your family and friends don't end up びょうき (byōki; sick) as well.

ガチガチ

Gachi-gachi

ガチガチ is used to describe the noise your body makes when the てんき (tenki; weather) is so cold your bones begin to *rattle* and the only thing you can think of saying is "*Brrrrrrr!*"

Human

Heartbeat

ドキドキ

Doki-doki

When you think about it, *thump-thump* doesn't really do justice to the sound of a racing heart. Not poetically, anyway. ドキドキ, on the other hand, is a perfect way to describe this shy schoolgirl's heartbeat when she spots a guy she thinks is かっこいい (kakkoii; cool).

どきっ

Doki

Here's another sound for the heart. But unlike the rapid-fire ドキドキ we heard above, a person's whose ticker goes どきっ is less anxious and more satisfied. Looks like he finally noticed her feelings for him. やった (yatta; yay)!

Human

Hunger

ぐぅきゅるるる

Guukyurururu

If you hear a *gurgle* in your stomach that sounds something like ぐうきゅるるる, it's time to put this book down and get yourself some grub. You've got the kind of hunger only a steaming bowl of カレーライス (karēraisu; curry rice) can cure!

ぺこぺこ

Peko-peko

Sometimes, you get so hungry that your tummy really begins to *rumble*. When you reach the point of ぺこぺこ, head straight to the nearest たべほうだい (tabehōdai; all-you-can-eat) restaurant.

Human

Jumping

ピョンピョン

Pyon-pyon

Looks like these girls are enjoying some なわとび (nawatobi; jump rope). Just like American girls, Japanese girls sing while they skip rope. But those songs aren't the only thing you'll hear – listen closely and you'll hear the ピョンピョン sound of jumping.

ぴょーん

Pyōn

An especially long jump gets the same sound – but hold the "o" to indicate this one is something special. ぴょーん! Think of it this way – the longer you extend the "o," the farther you ジャンプ (jampu; jump).

Human

Kissing

ちゅっ

Chu

PDAs (personal digital assistants) are common in Japan. The other kind of PDAs (public displays of affection) are not. But hey, はずかしがらないで (hazukashigaranaide; don't be shy)! You can get away with a little *smooch* – ちゅっ – on the cheek every now and then.

ブチュー

Buchuu

Not every kiss is welcome. Especially big, fat, sloppy ones that sound more like somebody sneezing – ブチュー – than smooching! So here our little friend is trying with all her might, but her love, alas, is unrequited.

Human

Laughter

あははは

Ahahaha

If *ahahaha* sounds familiar, it's because laughter is one sound that needs no translation, from トウキョウ (Tōkyō; Tokyo) to Ticonderoga. But in Japan, it's the boys who are most likely to let out a gut-busting あははは when they find something funny.

ホホホ / フォッフォッフォッ

Hohoho / Fuofuofuo

Ho-ho-ho, a sound we generally associate with Santa Claus, is more akin to a womanly *tee-hee-hee* to the Japanese. And フォッフォッフォッ is the sound of an elderly person (including Santa himself) making merry.

Human

Laziness

ごろごろ

Goro-goro

If you think relaxing with a comic book is a largely silent act ... you're wrong! The ごろごろ sound is associated with laziness. For instance, when you should be doing other things, such as helping your pushy おねえさん (onēsan; big sister) clean up the room!

だらだら

Dara-dara

Here's another sound for somebody who is kicking back when they probably should be hard at work. If you hear somebody going だらだら and ごろごろ at the same time, you've got a real lazybones on your hands.

Love

いちゃいちゃ

Icha-Icha

Who knew love could be heard beyond the heart? In Japan, it sounds a lot like いちゃいちゃ. Don't expect to hear it when you walk past a caring Japanese カップル (kappuru; couple), though. It's a sound only the lovers themselves can hear.

らぶらぶ

Rabu-rabu

らぶらぶ isn't a Japanese word for a massage – it's another onomatopoeia for love, this one coming direct from English. Because sometimes, you just can't help falling in らぶ (rabu; love)!

Mistake

オロオロ

Oro-oro

Forget *uh-oh!* When you've made a clumsy mistake in Japan, you're more likely to get an オロオロ. The sound usually, but not always, follows an おっとっと (ottotto; oops). That's when you'll want to learn the Japanese phrase for "It was already like that when I got here!"

わたわた

Wata-wata

When your arms flail and flap about as you try to cover up your mistake, it's likely to sound like わたわた. Of course, the more you わたわた, the more likely you'll be caught げんこうはん (genkōhan; red-handed)!

Muttering

ブツブツ

Butsu-butsu

Clearly, this boy is not having a good day at school. Maybe it's his friends giving him a hard time, low test scores, girl trouble, or mean teachers. It's enough to put a poor guy like him over the edge. Next thing you know, he's muttering – ブツブツ – to himself!

ぶーぶー

Buu-buu

The sound of disagreement is similar in English and Japanese. For instance, disgruntled fans at sports events often yell "*booooo!*" In this case, the boy clearly doesn't want to do his chores, and his ぶーぶー makes that quite clear!

Pain

キリキリ

Kiri-kiri

When it hurts – when it really, really hurts – you've got yourself some キリキリ. You may need to visit the びょういん (byōin; hospital), where a doctor can check you out. Injuries are unavoidable, though, when you lead a double life battling かいじゅう (kaijyuu; monsters)!

ズキンズキン

Zukin-zukin

Throbbing pain – the kind where you can feel your pulse inside of your injury, or when your tooth is banging on your jaw, trying to set itself free – is a little different. That's what the Japanese call ズキンズキン.

Human

Running

ダダダダダ

Dadadadada

Wow! Look at him go! すごい (sugoi; impressive)! To run with great haste, to approach on mere foot the speed of sound, is captured with a constant ダダダダダ. Each ダ is the sound of a foot quickly hitting the ground and then leaving it again just as fast.

たったったっ

Tattatta

Not everyone runs fast all the time. Shorter, slower strides more in line with a jog or a trot sound like たったったっ. This is just a little faster than the speed of regular あるき (aruki; walking).

Searching

キョロキョロ

Kyoro-kyoro

Look left. Look right. Look left again. You're not getting ready to cross the どうろ (dōro; street) – you've just got wandering eyes. The dead giveaway is the キョロキョロ that accompanies each glance. Wear your サングラス (sangurasu; sunglasses) next time, and no one will notice.

ウロウロ

Uro-uro

If wandering eyes sound like キョロキョロ, then ウロウロ describes actual wandering, along with some loitering and pacing. Just be sure to keep an eye out for oncoming traffic and errant pedestrians!

Sleepy

こっくり

Kokkuri

There are lots of places the world where you wouldn't dream of falling asleep on a train. Japan isn't one of them! The late trains home often have more than a few weary office workers going こっくり before they reach the しゅうてん (shuuten; last stop).

うとうと

Uto-uto

Here's an easier alternative: うとうと works just as well, especially when someone is nodding off while, say, reading a book. Hey, what are you doing? Don't fall asleep reading *this* book! おきて (okite; wake up)!

Human

Sleeping

すやすや

Suya-suya

Time to catch some *zzzs!* Or more precisely, すやすや in Japanese. Because homes in Japan's crowded cities are quite small, it's not uncommon for siblings to sleep and snore side by side – and sometimes entire families have to share a single bedroom.

ンゴーンガー

Ngō-ngaa

Not everyone gets a good night's sleep. ンゴーンガー is the uncomfortable sound made when you toss and turn all night. Good thing the ふとん (futon; Japanese bedding) is on the floor – at least you won't fall off!

Human

Slurping

ズルッ

Zuru

Japan is a place where manners rule. Even in the ラーメンやさん (ramenyasan; ramen restaurants), where patrons inhale their noodles with a constant, rhythmic, and very noisy ズルッズルッ. So feel free to *slurp* away – it's actually good manners!

ちゅるちゅる

Churu-churu

Here we have a quieter, and somewhat more delicate, version of slurping. Replacing a ズ or す with a ちゅ often feminizes a sound. In this case, though, both women and men can ちゅるちゅる their noodles.

Human

Smiling

ニコニコ

Niko-niko

Here's a student with something to be proud of. You can tell by the satisfied ニコニコ grin stretching across her face. Yes, she has just earned her そつぎょうしょうしょ (sotsugyōshōsho; diploma) – from Manga University, of course!

ニヤニヤ

Niya-niya

There are of course many kinds of smiles, from the モナリザ (Mona Riza; Mona Lisa) to the チェシャネコ (Chesha-neko; Cheshire Cat). A truly fiendish grin, though, comes across the face as ニヤニヤ. *Heh-heh-heh!*

Human

Sneaking

こそこそ

Koso-koso

You won't hear the こそこそ as the robber *creep-creeps* up, unless he's not very good at his job! There is something else interesting about this picture. This is the Japanese equivalent of a striped shirt and a black eye mask – a guise that cries out わるいひと (warui hito; bad guy)!

そろりそろり

Sorori-sorori

When the person doing the *tip-toeing* is far less sinister, you might hear そろりそろり instead. This boy is smart to let the sleeping dog lie; his bite is probably at least as bad as his bark.

Human

Sneezing

くしゅん

Kushun

The first sign that you may soon need to wear a マスク (masuku; mask) to prevent your friends from getting ill is a little くしゅん, a sort of abbreviated *achoo!* Just be sure to cover your くち (kuchi; mouth). That's polite in any culture!

ハックション

Hakkushon

A ハックション, on the other hand, is a room-stopping sneeze. The kind that makes people wonder if a じしん (jishin; earthquake) just hit. Note how the artist uses large, active kana around our sneezing pal. Stand back, he's gonna blow!

Human

Spinning

くるくる

Kuru-kuru

くるくるくるくる. Round and round she goes. How does she spin like that?! Check out her ゆうが (yuuga; grace) and みのこなし (minokonashi; poise). She skates like a champion; just like Shizuka Arakawa, Olympic gold medalist!

ぐるぐる

Guru-guru

Not everyone has the balance of a figure skater. Some people begin spinning so wildly, it's all they can do to keep from falling down. ぐるぐるぐるぐる. You can get めがまわる (megamawaru; dizzy) just looking at this picture!

Human

Staring

ジロジロ

Jiro-jiro

Poor boy! It's bad enough to have to wear a suit to school, but this lad is getting eyeballed by a teacher (or two!) checking to see if his がくらん (gakuran; schoolboy uniform) meets the dress code. The ジロジロ lets us know just how thorough this visual inspection is.

ちらっ

Chira

ちらっ is the noise made when one steals a quick glance, such as a shy おとこのこ (otokonoko; boy) checking out the cute おんなのこ (onnanoko; girl) sitting next to him on the train.

Human

Stretching

ぐにゃり

Gunyari

Not all of us have flexibility. Some of us have none at all. But for the lithe little gals gracing the pages of our favorite manga, a well-placed ぐにゃり lets us know they are as bendy as an オリンピック (orimpikku; Olympic) gymnast.

グキッ

Guki

For the rest of us, the *crack* of a グキッ lets everyone know the effort required to make the stretch. Note that the artist uses smooth, flowing characters for the fair maidens above, and sharp, rough kana for our less flexible friend.

Teeth

ギリギリ

Giri-giri

Biting your fingernails is a bad habit. ギリギリギリギリ is even worse. It could wear your teeth down, not to mention end your career as a にんじゃ (ninja), since it would reveal your position to your enemies. (By the way, ギリギリ also means "deadline.")

カチカチ

Kachi-kachi

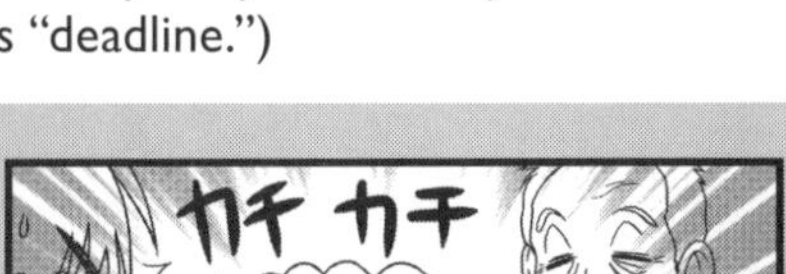

カチカチ is generally used to indicate the sound of two stones *banging* together. But as we can see, it's put to a more creative use here! *Clickety-clack*, don't bite back!

Human

Tickling

こちょこちょ

Kocho-kocho

Koochie-koochie koo! Or is that こちょこちょ to you? When you're the victim of a tickler, it probably doesn't matter. Let's just hope the tickling is a sign of affection! And in case you're wondering, わくわくドキドキ (waku-waku doki-doki) is the Japanese equivalent of "tickled pink."

こしょこしょ

Kosho-kosho

The lightest touch can often cause the biggest reaction. Like a little こしょこしょ on the bottom of the あし (ashi; foot). Note that this onomatopoeia has a softer sound than the more rigorous こちょこちょ. Now, *that* tickles!

Human

Tripping

コケッ

Koke

Oops! She didn't see that rock and, コケッ, down she goes. Who left an いし (ishi; stone) in the middle of the sidewalk anyway? Let's just hope that by the time this scene is finished, our friend hasn't landed flat on her pretty little かお (kao; face).

つるっ

Tsuru

If コケッ is best described as a "stumble and tumble," then つるっ is a "slip and slide." And as you can see from the illustration, banana peels are つるっ-type accidents waiting to happen in any language!

Human

Uneasy

ハラハラ

Hara-hara

You want to give someone the shivers? Introduce them to a few of your favorite ゆうれい (yuurei; Japanese monsters)! There's nothing like a late-night horror flick to fill a dark room with that on-the-edge-of-your-seat feeling the Japanese call ハラハラ. Boo!

ソワソワ

Sowa-sowa

There's another kind of uneasiness, the one when you really, really need to use the おべんじょ (obenjo), おといれ (otoire) or おてあらい (otearai) (all of which mean bathroom). Just say そわそわ and find the nearest stall!

Walking

とことこ

Toko-toko

Even at school, it's a Japanese custom to remove one's くつ (kutsu; shoes) at the door and replace them with うわばき (uwabaki; indoor shoes). And as these girls walk through the hall to their next class, there's the distinct sound of their hurried steps: とことことことこ.

スタスタ

Suta-suta

Japan is a very crowded country, and crisp individual footsteps are often lost as the number of feet pounding the pavement multiply. スタスタ is the sound of a crowd shuffling along as everyone heads to or from しごと (shigoto; work).

Human

Wrinkles

しわしわ

Shiwa-shiwa

The Japanese have the longest life expectancy in the world. Which explains why they also have an onomatopoeia, しわしわ, for wrinkles. Just tell the おばあさん (obaasan; old woman) and おじいさん (ojiisan; old man) that those are lines of distinction, not age!

シワシワ

Shiwa-shiwa

A shirt full of wrinkles gets the same sound, but here the artist uses the more angular katakana to make the distinction from the hiragana usage above. Maybe it's time to buy an アイロン (airon; iron).

Mechanical
sounds

きかい にかんする Onomatopoeia

Mechanical

Alarm clock

ピピピピピ

Pipipipipi

It always seems to happen this way. Just when you've finally managed to fall asleep – ピピピピピ! – the alarm clock goes off and it's time to wake up! And if it's a どようび (doyōbi; Saturday) morning and you could have slept in, the *beep-beep-beep* is even more bothersome.

ジリリリリ

Jiririririri

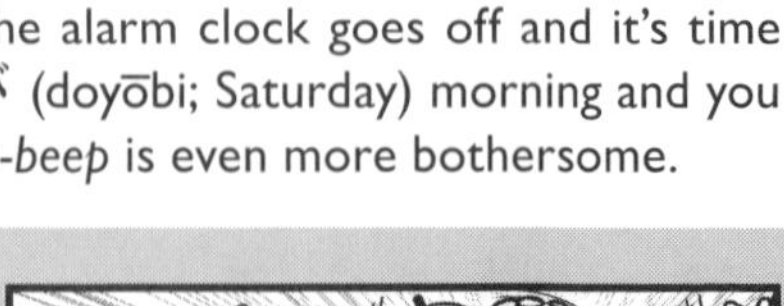

Modern-day めざましどけい (mezamashidokei; alarm clocks), with their digital readouts and fancy snooze buttons, are just too easy to ignore. Nothing says "wake up" like the ジリリリリ, or *ding-ding-ding-ding*, of a bell-style clock.

Mechanical

Automobile

ブロロロロ

Burororoor

The Japanese make some of the finest じどうしゃ (jidōsha; automobiles) in the world, so don't be surprised if the engine runs in near-silence. When you can hear it, though, it makes a satisfying ブロロロロ noise. *Vroooom!* That's the sound of quality!

キキイイイ

Kikiiii

The only thing more important to a くるま (kuruma; car) than a good set of wheels is a good set of ブレーキ (burēki; brakes). キキイイイ! *Screech!* That will teach you not to tailgate!

Bell

ゴーン

Gōn

ゴーン! *Gong!* At midnight on New Year's Eve, a monk rings a bell 108 times – one for each of what Buddhism defines as the 108 sins of man. This is called じょやのかね (Joya no Kane; New Year's Ringing of the Temple Bell), and allows people to start the year afresh.

カランカラン

Karan-karan

カランカラン! Looks like some lucky person just won the store からくじ (karakuji; raffle)! And to let everyone in the shop know, the clerk shakes a couple of hand bells in celebration. *Ring-a-ding!*

Mechanical

Chimes

キーンコーンカーンコーン

Kiin-kōn-kaan-kōn

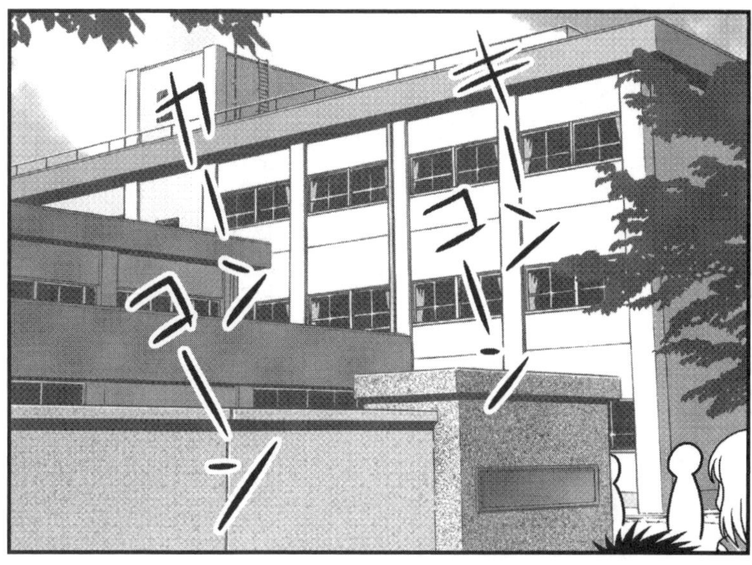

From Hokkaido to Okinawa, the Westminster Chimes can mean only one thing: school is in session! The tolling of large bells sounds almost the same in English and Japanese. *Ding-dong-dang-dong* – キンコンカンコン. Now hurry, you don't want to be late for class!

ピンポーン

Pin-pōn

The ピンポーン of a doorbell is a softer sound, with less of the *clang* associated with heavier bells. A Japanese teacher will make the same sound when a student answers a question correctly: "ピンポーン!" – "That's right!"

Mechanical

Electricity

ビリビリ

Biri-biri

Never! Touch! The! Plug! With! A! Wet! Hand! Looks like he didn't listen to his mother, and now he's being でんきショック (denkishokku; electrocuted). ビリビリビリ! *Bzzzzt!* Try to look on the "bright" side – he'll never need to buy another ランプ (rampu; lamp).

パチッ

Pachi

パチッ! *Zap!* Ouch! Don't you just hate that annoying せいでんき (seidenki; static electricity) in the winter time? But if this young lady thinks she got hurt, she should take a look at the guy above!

Mechanical

Guitar

ポロンポロン

Poron-poron

So you wanna be a J-rock 'n' roll star? Well, get yourself a ギター (gitaa; guitar) and start *twang-twangin'* away! To Japanese music lovers, ポロンポロン is the sound an acoustic six-stringer makes when it is being strummed. "Free Bird!" (Um, ask your parents...)

キュイイイン

Kyuiiin

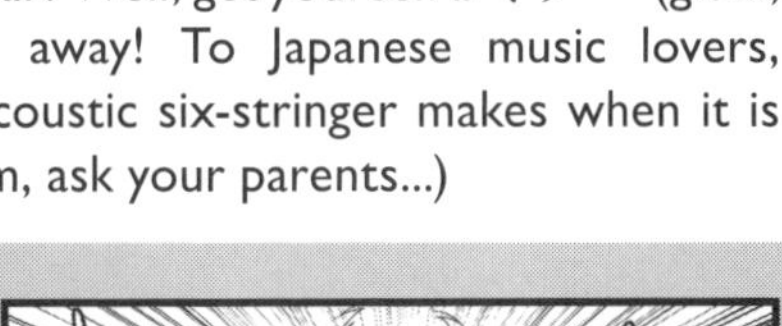

This guy is a pure ロッカー (rokka; rocker). He pours his heart and soul into the music as he attacks his axe. キュイイイン! Clearly his style is influenced more by X Japan and B'z than by Masayoshi Yamazaki. Rock on, bro'.

Mechanical

Gun

パンッパンッ

Pam-pan

Watch out, わるもの (warumono; bad guys)! Our ヒーロー (hiirō; hero) is packing heat, and he knows how to use it. パンッ! パンッ! *Bang-bang* (or, as we used to say, *pow-pow*)! A true manga hero never shoots to kill, of course. Unless he really, really has to.

ガガガガ

Gagagaga

The bigger the gun, the tougher the manga chick. ガガガガ – *ratatat-tat* – that mean-looking マシンガン (mashingan; machine gun) she's toting means serious business. Lock and load, baby!

Mechanical

Keyboard

カタカタ

Kata-kata

The sound of proficient hands タイピング (taipingu; typing) is almost musical. カタカタカタカタ. Forget a flowing river or a mountain breeze: there is something very ぜん (Zen)-like about the staccato *click-click-click* of a キーボード (kiibōdo; keyboard).

パチッ

Pachi

The ancient そろばん (soroban; abacus) still gets regular use in Japan. Walk into a local ぎんこう (ginkō; bank), and you're likely to hear the パチッパチッ *clickety-click* of the beads being counted on these old-time calculators.

Mechanical

Motorcycle

ベベベベベ

Bebebebebe

Motor scooters and their bigger cousins, motorcycles, or what the Japanese call オートバイ (ōtobai), are extremely popular with young people in Tokyo, Osaka and other crowded cities. At any given time, you can hear them *putt-putt-putting* down the streets, ベベベベベ.

ドドドドド

Dodododododo

Of course, a mere スクーター (skuutaa; scooter) isn't enough for this cool dude! No, he needs a turbocharged motorcycle, which will take him around town with a manly ドドドドド. *Vroooom!*

Mechanical

Robot

ガー

Gaa

In Japan, they're developing ロボット (robotto; robots) that will clean your house, cook your meals and – once they've tucked you safely into bed for the night – conquer the world. And as they do it, they'll make a noise that sounds something like ガーガー. You've been warned!

ジーコジーコ

Jiiko-jiiko

Wind-up おもちゃ (omocha; toys) have a mechanical sound all their own. They wobble along with a ジーコジーコ. Wouldn't it be something if, while we're all worried about giant robots, these little toys took over the world?

Mechanical

Train

ガタンゴトン

Gatan-goton

Japan has one of the most extensive and efficient rail systems in the world. Wherever you want to go, a でんしゃ (densha; train) can get you there. The ガタンゴトン, or *clickety-clack,* of the wheels on the tracks is a familiar sound throughout the nation. All aboard!

ポォーッ

Pō

What's a きかんしゃ (kikansha; locomotive) without its きてき (kiteki; whistle)? You can hear the powerful ポォーッ from miles away. Better clear the tracks – this iron horse has a schedule to keep!

Nature
sounds

しぜん にかんする **Onomatopoeia**

Nature

Boulder

ゴロンゴロン

Goron-goron

Every ぼうけんしゃ (bōkensha; adventurer) needs to keep his or her ears peeled for the ゴロンゴロン of a giant rolling おおいわ (ōiwa; boulder). In fact, as soon as you hear the sound – grab your hat and はしれ (hashire; run) like the wind!

コロコロ

Koro-koro

Oops. Someone missed the green, and the ball is rolling down toward the バンカー (bankaa; bunker, or sand trap). The softer コロコロ sound, though, tells us this ball is not heavy or dangerous like the boulder above.

Nature

Earthquake

グラグラ

Gura-gura

If you're used to standing on solid bedrock, it may be surprising to feel how often the ground shakes in Japan. When the bigger ones *rattle* your アパート (apaato; apartment), you'll hear the グラグラ as everything around you begins to ゆれる (yureru; shake).

ふらふら

Fura-fura

When you teeter on the がけ (gake; precipice), you might do your own frantic shaking. You'll probably flap your arms with a furious ふらふら. Good thing it's only the curb of the ほどう (hodō; sidewalk), so you won't fall far!

Fire

メラメラ

Mera-mera

Nothing beats a おくりび (okuribi; bonfire) on a cold night! Bonfires are a winter tradition at Manga University, just after the first snow. We all gather around as the fire *crackles*, メラメラ. Now, who wants to roast some マシュマロ (mashumaro; marshmallows)?

ボー

Bō

When the flames really begin to *roar*, the pleasant *crackle* vanishes and a frightening ボー takes its place. Looks like this かさい (kasai; fire) is out of control. Better call the しょうぼうしょ (shōbōsho; fire station)!

Nature

Heat

カラカラ

Kara-kara

Japan has only one desert, but it's almost 10 miles long, so it's possible an unlucky traveler could get lost. Just look at this guy. He's bone-dry, or カラカラ. Fortunately, there's probably a soda じどうはんばいき (jidōhanbaiki; vending machine) nearby, even out here!

カサカサ

Kasa-kasa

If you spend a hot summer day outdoors, you're likely to end up with a ひやけ (hiyake; sunburn or suntan). Dry skin is described as カサカサ, but try not to scratch it!

Nature

Rain

ザー

Zaa

It rains every now and then most anywhere you go. But in Japan, there is an entire つゆ (tsuyu; rainy season) between spring and summer. At some point nearly every day, you can count on hearing the sudden ザー of a downpour.

しとしと

Shito-shito

Individual しずく (shizuku; raindrops) fall with a gentle しとしと. The Japanese have a special doll-shaped charm called a てるてるぼず (teruterubozu) to ward off the rain – but this one, as Mr. Frog can attest, isn't working.

Nature

Snow

ヒュオオオオオ

Hyuooooo

There's ゆき (yuki; snow) and there's かぜ (kaze; wind). Put them together, and you get a full-blown ふぶき (fubuki; blizzard), complete with a nonstop *howl* that sounds like ヒュオオオオオ to the Japanese. Better wear earmuffs!

ちらほら

Chira-hora

The first snowflakes of winter fall with a gentle ちらほら, much to the delight of こどもたち (kodomotachi; children) everywhere. Let's just hope there's enough to build a ゆきだるま (yukidaruma; snowman).

Star

キラキラ

Kira-kira

キラキラひかる、よぞらのほしよ (kira-kira hikaru, yozora no hoshi yo)! C'mon, you know the song! *Twinkle, twinkle little star, how I wonder what you are.* Stars sparkle and shimmer with a キラキラ as they wink in and out across the night sky.

キラーン

Kiraan

When you look up at the よぞら (yozora; night sky) in many Japanese cities, you'll see only the brightest of the ほし (hoshi; stars), which shine through the light pollution with a steady キラーン.

Nature

Thunderstorm

ピカッ

Pika

Looks like Mother Nature is having a bad day! You can tell from the *flash* – ピカッ – of lightning overhead. Now head home and hide your belly button, because according to Japanese legend, かみなりさま (Kaminari-sama; God of Thunder) will try to steal it from you!

ゴロゴロ

Goro-goro

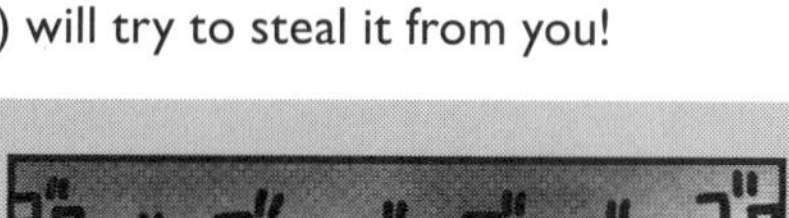

The distant *rumble* of ゴロゴロ is our first hint a らいう (raiu; thunderstorm) is rolling our way. The same onomatopoeia can be used to describe the sound made by other objects that roll, such as bowling balls and boulders.

Tree

ガサガサ

Gasa-gasa

あった (atta; there it is)! He's been looking for the ボール (bōru; ball) for 20 minutes now! As usual, it was hidden in the bushes. So the boy parts the leaves, which make a pleasant ガサガサ *rustle,* and soon the ball is back in play.

ザワザワ

Zawa-zawa

ザワザワ is another way to describe the rustle of leaves, but in this case we are talking not about a little bush, but the expanded sound of a windswept もり (mori; forest).

Nature

Volcano

どっかーん

Dokkaan

Japan sits on the edge of the Ring of Fire, the world's most active chain of かざん (kazan; volcanoes). If you happen to live near one, you might want to flee at the first rumbles – don't stick around to hear the どっかーん, or *kaboom,* of the eruption!

どろどろ

Doro-doro

Some of Japan's volcanoes, such as Sakurajima, are active on an almost daily basis, with regular ようがん (yōgan; lava) flows. If you're brave enough to get close, you'll hear どろどろ as it *oozes* its way down the mountain.

Nature

Water

ジャー

Jyaa

Washing your て (te; hands) regularly with soap and warm water will kill most of the germs you encounter each day. So if you happen to be a バイキン (baikin; germ), there is perhaps no sound as terrifying as the steady stream of water from a faucet – ジャー!

ピチャン

Pichan

A drop of dew falling from a leaf is the perfect element for a classic はいく (haiku; Japanese poem). And the gentle sound it makes? ピチャン. Now go write some poetry that would make Bashō proud!

Nature

Waves

ザザーン

Zazaan

Many Japanese live near the かいよう (kaiyō; sea), so the relaxing ザザーン of the gentle waves is a familiar sound. For those lucky residents, there's no need to buy one of those nature-sound CDs to help lull themselves to sleep!

ザッパーン

Zappaan

There are なみ (nami; waves) and then there are つなみ, or what you may know as "tsunami." These monstrous towers of water rise with a furious sound all their own: ザッパーン!

Nature

Wind

ビュー

Byuu

This manga, my friend, is blowing in the wind. And it looks like a pretty stiff じんぷう (jinpuu; gust), too. If the flowing かみのけ (kaminoke; hair) isn't a dead giveaway, the ビュー sound is. In English, we use the word *whoosh* to signify the same thing.

そよそよ

Soyo-soyo

A more gentle breeze flows with an almost-silent そよそよ. This little cat closes her eyes against the かぜ (kaze; wind). Or maybe she's just taking a ひるね (hirune; catnap).

Other
sounds

そのたのOnomatopoeia

Other

Barbecue

ジュージュー

Jyuu-jyuu

Forget すし (sushi) for a minute. The Japanese also love to barbecue. But instead of thick, American-sized ステーキ (sutēki; steaks), they tend to grill thin, tender cuts of beef and vegetables. The ジュージュー of the *sizzle* on the grill is enough to make anyone's mouth water.

グツグツ

Gutsu-gutsu

Not in the mood for meat? No problem, we'll make a seafood soup instead. Once we've got a good グツグツ boil going, we'll add the やさい (yasai; vegetables) and maybe some めん (men; noodles). おいしい (oishii; yummy)!

Other

Burn

ヒリヒリ

Hiri-hiri

Ouch! That's あつい (atsui; hot)! A burn is a very special kind of pain known as ヒリヒリ. It's an everyday hazard of living in Japan, where boiling-hot cups of おちゃ (ocha; green tea) are served just about everywhere.

ピリピリ

Piri-piri

A scrape also has a burning sensation, as anyone who's skinned a ひざ (hiza; knee) can attest. So there's no surprise that it sounds a lot like a regular burn: ピリピリ.

Other

Drip

ポタンポタン

Potan-potan

We've got a leak – and a pretty big one too! Someone better call the かんりにんさん (kanrininsan; building superintendent) before the slow-but-steady ポタンポタン of the drops turns into an uncontrollable rush of water and the pan overflows.

ポタポタ

Pota-pota

Here's a much more urgent *drip-drop* sound – if you're in need of a quick caffeine fix! The コーヒー (kōhii; coffee) drips into the pot with a reassuring ポタポタ. Just a few more minutes till java-time!

Other

Explosion

ドーン

Dōn

This is one of our specialties at Manga University. After all, what's a comic book without a big explosion? In English, we say *boom, kaboom,* and sometimes even *kablooey.* In Japanese, though, a single, loud ドーン gets the job done. That was cool!

ガガガ

Gagaga

When you hear a loud ガガガ at a construction site, expect to see some heavy machinery blast through the rock at any moment. And if you live near the construction site, you'll probably be ready to go gaga!

Other

Fluffy

ふわふわ

Fuwa-fuwa

It's good to be a てんし (tenshi; angel). You get to spend your days floating around on fluffy white clouds as they drift ふわふわ across the heavens. Just remember to remain on the lookout for little あくま (akuma; devils)!

もこもこ

Moko-moko

Even though December 25 isn't an official holiday in Japan, many Japanese children still expect to receive toys on クリスマス (kurisumasu; Christmas) morning from the man in the もこもこ – fluffy – red suit.

Other

Flutter

パタパタ

Pata-pata

Across Japan, students gather each autumn to compete in うんどうかい (undōkai; school athletic meets). Their parents show up in the wee hours of the あさ (asa; morning) so they have a good seat when the team flags are raised and *flap* in the wind with a パタパタ.

ヒラヒラ

Hira-hira

The Japanese never leave home without a ハンカチ (hankachi; handkerchief). Perfect for when you need to くしゃみ (kushami; sneeze), dry your hands – or, like this young gal, call your friends over with a ヒラヒラ as you wave it about.

Other

Knock

トントン

Ton-ton

トントン. *Knock-knock.*
だれ (dare; who's there)?
べん (ben; Ben). なにべん (nani ben; Ben who)?
べんきょうしましょう (benkyōshimashō; let's study)!

ドンドン

Don-don

A loud, urgent ドンドン on the door requires the immediate attention of anyone inside. *Bam-bam!* He's sure going to be はずかしい (hazukashii; embarrassed) when he realizes he's at the wrong house!

Other

Luxury

しゃなりしゃなり

Shanari-shanari

Here's a びしょうじょ (bishōjo; beautiful girl) who's the toast of the town. There is a shimmering noise – しゃなりしゃなり – as she waltzes into the room, and every head turns her way. Let's just hope she makes it home before the stroke of よなか (yonaka; midnight)!

キラキラ

Kira-kira

Check out all the ひかりもの (hikarimono; shiny stuff) she's wearing! You can tell from the sparkles – キラキラ – that her *bling-bling* is the real deal. Forget "Breakfast at Tiffany's." This girl had lunch and dinner there, too!

Other

Paper

バラバラ

Bara-bara

From out of nowhere comes a gust of wind, and the sheets of かみ (kami; paper) make a rustling noise, バラバラ, as they are blown away in all directions. She'll just have to tell the teacher that Mother Nature ate her しゅくだい (shukudai; homework)!

ごちゃごちゃ

Gocha-gocha

These papers are in no danger of going anywhere. They've been in this ごちゃごちゃ mess for ages. It seems like all she ever does is move them from one やま (yama; pile) to another.

Other

Shatter

パリン

Parin

Washing dishes is a thankless job. That's the second さら (sara; plate) she's dropped tonight, and everyone in the restaurant heard the パリン sound as the glass shattered on the floor. Maybe she's trying to get herself fired!

ガシャンッ

Gashan

Darn cat! It jumped right out of the boy's arms and onto the antique かびん (kabin; vase), sending it to the ground with a loud ガシャンッ. Wait till mom gets home – that vase isn't the only thing that's going to be busted!

Other

Silence

ちょこんっ

Chokon

In Japan, even silence has a sound. For instance, this little girl is camped out on the floor, ちょこんっ, quietly minding her own business. She's so still and silent she almost got stepped on! あぶないよ (abunai yo; be careful)! These guys need to watch where they step!

ぽつん

Potsun

One delicate flower, sitting in a windswept field all by itself. How did it even get there? It sure looks さびしい (sabishii; lonely)! ぽつん is another way to express the sound of silence.

Other

Slip/Slide

ズポッ

Zupo

It's a classic comic-book scene: A happy-go-lucky キャラ (kyara; character) is walking down the street at a brisk pace, minding his own business, when suddenly: ズポッ! Somebody left the マンホール (manhōru; manhole) uncovered, and he sinks right in!

すぽっ

Supo

The season's first snow is falling, which means it's time to wear boots. She slides her foot in, gives it a wiggle and – すぽっ – it slips right on. Now she's all set for ふゆやすみ (fuyuyasumi; winter vacation)!

Other

Splinter

バキッ

Baki

Don't mess with this little からて (karate) master. As you can see, he's very つよい (tsuyoi; strong). And in case you couldn't tell from his black belt, he just shattered a board with a loud バキッ – *crack* – to let everyone know what he's capable of!

ポキッ

Poki

A more gentle break requires a softer sound. The tip of her pencil went ポキッ – *snap* – just as she began taking the にゅうがくしけん (nyuugakushiken; entrance exam). That certainly can't be a good sign!

Other

Steam

シューッ

Shuu

As any Japanese will tell you, when you have おゆ (oyu; hot water), you're only さんぷん (sampun; 3 minutes) away from a hot meal. Once you hear the シューッ from the kettle, just add the hot water to your instant noodles and your hunger will soon be history.

ブクブク

Buku-buku

Don't try cooking your meal in a ガスバーナー (gasubaanaa; gas burner, or, more accurately, Bunsen burner), though! What sounds like *blub-blub-blub* to Western ears is ブクブク in Japanese.

Other

Sticky

べたべた

Beta-beta

Don't you just it hate when this happens? You open a can of コーラ (cōra; cola) and the beverage fizzes over the top, over your hands and down your arm, leaving you with that sticky べたべた feeling. What a mess!

べとーっ

Betō

Even worse than spilling soda all over yourself is when you land your foot into some ガム (gamu; chewing gum), and べトーっ – every step you take becomes a long and sticky one!

Wet

びしょびしょ

Bisho-bisho

Hey, accidents happen. So why does she look so miserable? Probably because that was nasty water from a モップ (moppu; mop). Yuck! Now she's got a soaking-wet びしょびしょ mess on her hands – and has to start her そうじ (sōji; cleaning) all over again.

ぼたぼた

Bota-bota

Looks like the girl above isn't the only one having trouble finishing her chores. This boy is trying to wring the extra water out of his ぞうきん (zōkin; rag), but it's ぼたぼた – *drip-drip* dripping – everywhere!

INDEX OF SOUNDS